DORSET
COUNTRY RECIPES

COMPILED BY
PIPPA GOMAR

RAVETTE BOOKS

Published by Ravette Limited,
3 Glenside Estate, Star Road,
Partridge Green, Horsham,
Sussex RH13 8RA
(0403) 710392

Production: Oval Projects Ltd.
Cover Design: Jim Wire
Printing & binding: Nørhaven AS

All recipes are given in Imperial and Metric
weights and measures. Where measurements
are given in 'cups', these are American cups,
holding 8 fluid ounces.

The recipes contained in this book are traditional
and many have been compiled from archival sources.
Every effort has been made to ensure that the recipes
are correct.

RECIPES

SAVOURIES

SALADS and VEGETABLES

PUDDINGS

DORSET

Dorset is an unspoiled county of rolling hills, valleys and heaths, while its long coastline and numerous rivers yield many delicious varieties of marine and freshwater fish. It is also Thomas Hardy country. This well-known writer and poet was born in High Brockhampton in 1840, and his novels provide a fascinating insight into country life in the 19th century.

Farming has always been one of the county's main activities; sheep flourish on the hills, while the wide and fertile valleys support large herds of cows and rich crops of wheat and fruit. Dorset is famous for its dairy products, in particular its cream, butter and the elusive Blue Vinney cheese, a blue-veined cheese made from low fat milk, probably the left-overs from butter and cheese-making. Sherborne is reputed to be the centre of the Blue Vinney country, and although only a few places still make the cheese, it is so delicious that it is well worth the effort of tracking it down. A more commonly found cheese nowadays is the blue-veined Dorset Blue.

Cheese was frequently eaten with Dorset Knobs, which are crisp, rusk-like rolls. They are still made in the traditional, labour-intensive way - which involves baking them twice - by the family-run Moores' Bakery in Morcombelake.

Also peculiar to the county are Dorset Horned Sheep. This breed is unusual in being able to produce lambs at any time of the year, so even before refrigeration, it was possible to eat fresh lamb out of season. Indeed roast lamb was a popular meat for Christmas dinner in the 18th and 19th centuries. Another favourite throughout the year was Lamb's Tail Pie, which is a dish of lambs' tails with bacon, hard-boiled eggs, herbs, lemon rind and stock, covered with a pastry crust.

In the days when some families kept their own pigs to be fattened for the table, no part of the animal was wasted. What could not be eaten straight away was salted down for the winter, a long process which took several days, or even weeks, to complete. And those parts which could not be salted down were made into brawn, sausages, pies, 'black pot' (black pudding) and lard.

Pickled vegetables provided a welcome variety of food during the winter, as, too, did the plentiful fruit preserved as marmalades, jams, jellies and chutneys.

Apples have always been widely grown in Dorset. At least 25 different and strange-sounding varieties are known to have been cultivated in the 19th century, some being particularly popular in certain districts. Cat's Head and Smell Mary were plentiful around Bridport, while Sweet Acum and Bloody Butcher were found in Marshwood Vale, and Sheep's Nose (or Bishop's Nose) and Grindstone in East Chelborough. Other varieties, such as Slack-Ma-Girdle, Fox Whelp, Iron Apple and Bell Ringer were common in all districts. Not unnaturally, cider, called 'Scrumpie' throughout the whole of the West Country, was, and still is, a popular drink, made and consumed in the home as well as in the county's attractive inns. Dorset Ale, famous for its strength, was described by Thomas Hardy as:

"...of the most beautiful colour as the eye of an artist in beer could desire; full in body yet brisk as a volcano; piquant, yet without a twang; luminous as an Autumn sunset; free from streakiness of taste, but finally, rather heady."

Today the Dorchester Brewer, Eldridge Pope, produce a good strong ale which Hardy would have recognised - and enjoyed!

There is much of great historical interest in the county, and as well as that, visitors should take every opportunity to sample the traditional Dorset fare which is now widely available in the charming hotels, restaurants and inns in this most beautiful of English counties.

'If you in Do'set be a-roamen,
An' ha' business at a farm
Then woon't ye see your eale a-foamen,
Or your cider down to warm?
Woon't ye have brown bread a-put ye?
An' some venny cheese ent ye?
Butter? Rolls o't!
Cream? Why bowls o't!'

Reverend William Barnes
(Dorset poet 1800 - 86)

WATERCRESS WITH CREAM CHEESE

Serves 4

8 oz (225 g) cream cheese
3 oz (75 g) flaked almonds
2 oz (50 g) butter
1 bunch watercress

For the French dressing:
2 tablespoons olive oil
1 tablespoon vinegar
1 teaspoon French mustard
Salt and pepper

To make the watercress with cream cheese:

Divide the cream cheese into 20 pieces.

Roll each piece into a ball and chill.

Saute the flaked almonds in the butter until golden brown.

Drain on kitchen towelling.

Wash the watercress.

Discard yellow leaves and coarse stalks.

Arrange the watercress on four small plates.

Put five balls of cream cheese on to each watercress bed.

Sprinkle with the almonds.

Spoon the dressing over just before serving.

To make the French dressing:

Whisk the oil and the vinegar together until it has thickened and is cloudy.

Add salt and pepper to taste.

Add the mustard and whisk again.

1

BUTTERED CRAYFISH

Serves 6 as a beginning to a meal

Crayfish are freshwater shell fish, rather like small lobsters. They turn red like lobsters when cooked. Many streams in Dorset were once full of crayfish but are now seriously depleted. Prawns may be used in this recipe instead of crayfish.

12 oz (350 g) crayfish
3 oz (75 g) butter
2 tablespoons water
2 tablespoons white wine
A blade of mace
A pinch of salt
Half a lemon

Put the water, wine, mace and a pinch of salt into a saucepan.

Add a pared strip of peel from the lemon.

Bring to the boil and simmer for about 5 minutes.

Put in the crayfish and simmer until they are hot and cooked (the flesh will turn pink/red).

Add the butter.

When the butter has melted, add the juice of $^1/_2$ lemon.

Serve on a bed of watercress.

SCALLOPED CRAB

Serves 6

This 18th century dish makes a good beginning for a dinner, served in scallop shells.

3 small dressed crabs
2 oz (50 g) butter
4 oz (100 g) white breadcrumbs
Salt and pepper
Cayenne pepper
$^1/_2$ teaspoon mace
The juice of half a lemon
3 anchovies
2 oz (50 g) cheese

Melt the butter.

Chop the crab meat and add to the melted butter.

Add the breadcrumbs, salt, pepper , mace and a pinch of cayenne pepper. Mix well.

Add the lemon juice.

Chop the anchovies and add to the mixture.

Heat gently, stirring to prevent the mixture sticking to the bottom of the pan.

Heat the grill.

Put the mixture into 6 scallop shells.

Sprinkle with finely grated cheese.

Put under the grill to brown.

Serve immediately or put in a low oven to keep warm for not longer than 15 minutes.

POTTED HERRINGS

3 fresh herrings
6 oz (175 g) butter
$^{1}/_{2}$ teaspoon cayenne pepper
$^{1}/_{2}$ teaspoon powdered mace
12 fl oz (350 ml/ 1$^{1}/_{2}$ cups) cider
A pinch of salt

Remove the heads and tails of the herrings.

Scale the fish by scraping with a knife from head to tail.

Gut the fish.

Put the herrings into a saucepan with the cider.

Simmer gently for 20-30 minutes.

Drain and discard the cider, reserving 2 tablespoonsful.

Remove all the bones and skin from the herrings.

Mash the flesh.

Return to the saucepan with half the butter, the cayenne pepper, mace, a pinch of salt and 2 tablespoons of fish stock/cider.

Stir well, and heat gently.

Put the mixture into 6 small pots or 1 large one.

Leave to cool.

Melt the remaining butter and pour over the potted fish.

Chill, then serve with melba toast.

WATERCRESS SOUP

There are extensive watercress beds outside Bere Regis. These rely on artesian wells which go 100 feet below the chalk for the water that bubbles under its own pressure at a constant temperature of 50°C throughout the year.

1 onion
4 oz (100 g) watercress
8 oz (225 g) potatoes
2 oz (50 g) butter
$^{1}/_{4}$ pint (150 ml/ $^{2}/_{3}$ cup) single cream
1 pint (600 ml/ 2$^{1}/_{2}$ cups) stock (a chicken stock cube may
   be used)
Salt and pepper

Peel and dice the potatoes.

Wash the watercress, discarding any yellow leaves and coarse stalks.

Chop the onion and fry in the butter until soft but not brown.

Add the stock, potatoes and watercress.

Bring to the boil and simmer for about 30 minutes.

Season the soup with salt and pepper.

Blend the soup in a liquidizer or work through a wire sieve.

Add the cream and re-heat gently but be careful it does not boil or the cream will curdle.

Serve immediately with croutons.

APPLE SOUP

3 large cooking apples
1 oz (25 g) butter
1 oz (25 g) flour
1 onion
4 cloves
1 oz (25 g) sugar
Salt and pepper
2 pints (1.15 litres/ 5 cups) milk and water
    (half and half)

Peel, core and slice the apples.

Melt the butter in a large saucepan.

Fry the apples in the butter for a few minutes.

Add the flour and cook for a few minutes.

Gradually add the milk and water.

Add the sugar and a little salt and pepper.

Cut the onion in half and stick each half with cloves.

Put the onion halves into the soup.

Cover the pan and simmer for 1 hour.

Remove the onion halves and the cloves.

Serve the soup either hot or cold.

RED MULLET

Serves 4

Weymouth was renowned for its red mullet during the 19th century. In the 19th century the then Duke of Portland used to visit the town especially to dine on this fish.

4 large or 8 small red mullet
2 oz (50 g) flour
Half an onion
1 teaspoon chopped parsley
1 teaspoon chopped fennel
4 mushrooms
4 tablespoons sherry
1 oz (25 g) butter
Salt
A little cayenne pepper

Clean the fish and remove only the gills.

Cut pieces of foil big enough to wrap each fish separately.

Butter the foil.

Put a fish in the middle of each piece of foil.

Slice the onion.

Chop the mushrooms.

Divide the onion, parsley, fennel, mushrooms and sherry equally between the fish parcels.

Sprinkle the fish with salt and cayenne pepper.

Make a double fold in the foil on the top of the fish and at the ends to secure well and keep all the juices in.

Put the fish parcels into a baking tin.

Bake for 30 minutes.

Serve the fish in the foil, or on a hot dish with melted butter and a slice of lemon.

Oven: 350°F/180°C Gas Mark 4

7

TENCH WITH HERBS

Tench live in shallow ponds or lakes.

4 tench
1 onion
Salt and pepper
Oil
1 tablespoon finely chopped parsley

Wash and gut the fish.

Put the fish in a pan and cover with water.

Bring to the boil and cook for a few minutes.

Remove the fish from the water, dry them and remove the scales by running a knife from tail to head.

Lay the fish in a deep dish.

Chop the onion and sprinkle on top of the fish.

Add the parsley and season with salt and pepper.

Pour in enough oil to cover the fish.

Leave to marinade for 2 hours.

Remove and wrap each fish individually in foil.

Put in pre-heated oven for 15 minutes.

Serve in the foil or on a hot dish, with lemon slices and mustard.

Oven: 400°F/200°C Gas Mark 6

BAKED MACKEREL

Serves 4

4 small mackerel
$^{1}/_{4}$ pint (150 ml/ $^{2}/_{3}$ cup) white wine vinegar
$^{1}/_{4}$ pint (150 ml/ $^{2}/_{3}$ cup) cider
Salt and pepper
A few cloves
Half a nutmeg, grated

Scale and gut the fish.

Scrape out the inside of the belly and rub the cavity with salt.

Cut off the fins.

Remove the head just behind the gills.

Put the mackerel in a shallow dish.

Pour on the wine vinegar and the cider.

Add a few cloves.

Sprinkle with grated nutmeg, salt and pepper.

Cover the dish with foil.

Bake for 30-40 minutes.

Serve either hot or cold.

Oven: 350°F/180°C Gas Mark 4

MARINADED FISH

Lampreys, eels, mackerel, trout or salmon steaks may be cooked this way.

4 fish or 4 salmon steaks
2 oz (50 g) flour
1 oz (25 g) butter
A little oil
$^1/_4$ pint (150 ml/ $^2/_3$ cup) white wine vinegar
$^1/_4$ pint (150 ml/ $^2/_3$ cup) white wine
1 onion, sliced
A pinch of cinnamon
A sprig of rosemary
1 bay leaf
Salt and pepper
1 lemon

Clean, scale, gut and remove the heads of the fish.

Score each fish to make slits along the back.

Roll the fish in the flour.

Heat the oil and the butter in a large frying pan and brown the fish.

Lower the heat and finish cooking the fish slowly for about 5minutes on each side.

Remove the fish from the pan and leave to cool.

Meanwhile gently boil the vinegar, wine, sliced onion, cinnamon, rosemary, bay leaf, salt and pepper in a saucepan for about 15 minutes.

Put the fish in a shallow dish and pour the marinade over.

Leave overnight.

Drain and serve with sliced lemon.

TO STEW CARP

Serves 4-6

Recipes for stewing carp appear over and over again in 18th and 19th century recipe books, suggesting that carp must have been a major catch in the Dorset rivers.

$2^{1}/_{2}$-3 lb (1.25-1.5 kg) carp
$^{1}/_{4}$ pint (150 ml/ $^{2}/_{3}$ cup) white wine
$^{1}/_{4}$ pint (150 ml/ $^{2}/_{3}$ cup) water
1 onion, sliced
1 oz (25 g) butter
1 teaspoon anchovy essence
Mixed herbs
A few cloves
Half a nutmeg
2 blades of mace

Scale and gut the carp. Rub the cavity with salt.

Soak the carp in heavily salted water for 3 hours.

Drain and put the fish in a large saucepan.

Add the wine, water and sliced onion.

Put the herbs, cloves, nutmeg and mace in a muslin bag and put into the saucepan with the fish and the liquid.

Simmer gently for 20-30 minutes or until fish is tender.

Remove the fish and keep warm.

Retain the fish stock.

In another pan melt the butter until it is brown.

Gradually add about $^{1}/_{4}$ pint (150 ml/ $^{2}/_{3}$ cup) of the fish stock.

Add the anchovy essence and heat until the sauce has thickened.

Pour the sauce over the carp and serve.

RABBIT FRIED WITH ONIONS

Serves 4

In the 16th, 17th and 18th centuries domestic rabbits, known as 'coneys', were kept in enclosed warrens and fattened for 2 weeks in a hutch before being killed and eaten. Poorer people had to make do with wild rabbits.

2¹/₂ lbs (1.25 kg) rabbit
2 or 3 eggs
About 8 oz (225 g) breadcrumbs
Salt and pepper
4 oz (100 g) butter
4 onions
¹/₂ tablespoon flour
¹/₂ pint (300 ml/ 1¹/₄ cups) stock
1 tablespoon lemon juice
6 tablespoons single cream

Joint the rabbit. Put the pieces into a large pan of boiling water for a few minutes.

Drain and cool.

Beat the eggs.

Season the breadcrumbs with salt and pepper and spread on to a plate.

Dip the rabbit joints first in the egg then into the breadcrumbs.

Fry the rabbit joints gently in half the butter until they are brown all over (about 15 minutes).

Slice the onion into rings.

In a second frying pan fry the onion rings gently in the remaining butter until they are soft.

Put the onions on to a large serving plate and keep warm.

Put the rabbit joints on top of the onions.

Stir the flour into any remaining juices from the two pans.

Pour in the stock and cook gently until it has thickened.

Just before serving, stir in the lemon juice and the cream, but do not re-heat.

Serve the sauce with the rabbit and onions, accompanied by mashed or creamed potato, and beans or spinach.

DORSET RABBIT

1 jointed rabbit
1 oz (25 g) flour
A little salt and freshly ground pepper
4 oz (100 g) streaky bacon
$^1/_4$ pint (150 ml/ $^2/_3$ cup) cider

For the topping:
4 oz (100 g) shredded suet
8 oz (225 g) fresh breadcrumbs
2 onions
Grated rind of $^1/_2$ lemon
1 teaspoon dried sage
1 beaten egg
A little milk

Blanch the rabbit joints in boiling water, then pat dry.

Season the flour with salt and pepper.

Roll the rabbit in the seasoned flour. Put in a casserole dish.

Lay the bacon rashers on the rabbit and pour the cider over.

Mix the suet, breadcrumbs, grated lemon rind and dried sage.

Chop the onion finely and mix it in.

Bind the mixture with beaten egg and a little milk.

Cover the rabbit with the topping. Cover and cook for 2 hours.

Remove the lid and continue cooking for about 20 minutes to brown the topping.

Oven: 350°F/180°C Gas Mark 4

POACHER'S PIE

2 small rabbits
3 eggs
1 oz (25 g) cornflour

For the pastry:
6 oz (175 g) flour
3 oz (75 g) butter
A pinch of salt
A little water

Skin and joint the rabbits.

Put them into a large saucepan and cover with water.

Simmer gently for 2 hours, covered.

Hard-boil the eggs and slice them.

Line a fairly large pie dish with the eggs.

When the rabbit is tender, remove the joints from the saucepan and put them into the pie dish on top of the eggs.

Thicken the stock in the saucepan with cornflour.

To make the pastry:

Sieve the flour and salt together.

Rub in the butter until the mixture resembles breadcrumbs. Add enough cold water to make a soft dough.

Roll out the pastry and cover the pie dish with it, dampening the edges to seal. Use any left-over pastry to make leaf shapes for decoration.

Bake for 25 minutes or until the pastry is golden brown. Serve cold.

Oven: 400°F/200°C Gas Mark 6

OLD ENGLISH LAMB

1 leg of lamb-about 3 lbs (1.4 kg)
$\frac{1}{2}$ oz (15 g) lard
1$\frac{1}{2}$-2 lbs (675 g-1 kg) potatoes
1 orange
1 tablespoon clear honey
A pinch of salt
1 tablespoon flour
$\frac{1}{2}$ pint (300 ml/ 1$\frac{1}{4}$ cups) stock
A few sprigs of mint

Peel the potatoes and parboil them for about 5 minutes.

Score the lamb in a criss-cross pattern.

Put the lamb, lard and potatoes into a roasting tin.

Grate the rind of the orange.

Mix the orange rind, honey and a pinch of salt in a bowl, and spread the mixture over the meat.

Roast in the oven for 2 hours, basting occasionally.

Put the meat and potatoes on to a serving dish and keep warm.

Make a sauce by stirring the flour and stock into the meaty juices left in the pan.

Boil until it has thickened.

Peel the orange and remove the pith.

Cut across into 6 slices.

Serve the lamb with the sauce and garnish with the orange slices and sprigs of mint.

Oven: 350°F/180°C Gas Mark 4

SPICED MUTTON

Serves 4-6

Cabbages, which are an important ingredient of this recipe, were introduced into Dorset from Holland in the 17th century.

2 lbs (1 kg) boned mutton (loin, leg or shoulder are suitable)
2 oz (50 g) oatmeal
1/4 teaspoon dried thyme
1/2 teaspoon black pepper
A pinch of mace
2 oz (50 g) lard
Large cabbage leaves from a savoy cabbage
1/2 pint (300 ml/ 1 1/4 cups) cider
1/4 pint (150 ml/ 2/3 cup) red wine

Mix the oatmeal, thyme, black pepper and mace.

Roll the meat in the seasoned oatmeal, rubbing it in well.

Tie up the joint.

Cover with lard cut up into small pieces.

Wrap the meat in the cabbage leaves making sure it is completely covered.

Put the meat in a roasting tin.

Baste with the cider.

Roast for 50 minutes basting occasionally with the cider.

Pour off the excess fat, remove the cabbage leaves and pour the red wine over the meat.

Continue cooking for another 40 minutes, basting occasionally.

Serve with the juices from the pan, a watercress salad and redcurrant jelly.

Oven: 350°F/180°C Gas Mark 4

PORTLAND PASTIES

Pasties are very popular in the West country.

For the pastry:
1 lb (450 g) flour
8 oz (225 g) butter
$^1/_2$ teaspoon salt
A little water

For the filling:
8 oz (225 g) minced beef
12 oz (350 g) turnips
8 oz (225 g) potatoes
1 tablespoon horseradish sauce
1 beaten egg to glaze

To make the pastry:

Sieve the flour and the salt together.

Rub in the butter until the mixture resembles breadcrumbs.

Add enough cold water to make a soft dough.

Roll out the pastry thinly.

Cut out 8 circles about 6 inches (15 cm) in diameter.

To make the filling:

Grate the turnips.

Peel and dice the potatoes.

Mix together the minced beef, turnip, potato and horseradish sauce.

Divide the mixture equally between the pastry circles, putting it in the middle of each circle.

Wet the edges of the pastry.

Fold each circle in half and crimp the edges.

Brush each pasty with beaten egg.

Make a small hole in the top of each pasty to let out the steam.

Bake for 15 minutes at the higher temperature.

Lower the oven temperature and bake for a further 30 minutes, until golden brown.

Oven: 400°F/200°C Gas Mark 6
Reduce to: 350°F/180°C Gas Mark 4

DORSET JUGGED STEAK

Serves 4

Jugging is simply a method of cooking meat slowly in liquid until it is very tender.

1¹/₂ lbs (675 g) braising steak
1 oz (25 g) plain flour
1 onion
6 cloves
¹/₄ pint (150 ml/ ²/₃ cup) port
Beef or chicken stock (enough to cover the meat)
Salt and pepper
1 tablespoon chopped parsley
4 oz (100 g) sausagemeat
4 oz (100 g) breadcrumbs
1 egg
1 tablespoon redcurrant jelly

Cut the steak into cubes removing any excess fat or gristle.

Roll the meat in the flour and place in a casserole dish.

Stick the cloves into the onion and add to the casserole, add the chopped parsley, port and enough stock to cover the meat completely. Season to taste with salt and pepper.

Put the lid on the casserole dish and cook gently in the oven for about 2-2¹/₂ hours, topping up with stock if necessary.

Meanwhile mix together the sausagemeat and the breadcrumbs. Add the beaten egg to bind.

Roll the mixture into small balls with floured hands.

Boil the sausagemeat balls in water for about 10 minutes.

Lift them out and add to the casserole with the redcurrant jelly 15 minutes before the end of the cooking time. Leave the lid off for the final 15 minutes.

Remove the onion and the cloves before serving.

Oven: 300°F/150°C Gas Mark 2

DORSET SAUSAGE

Serves 8

This is more like a meat loaf than a sausage. It is eaten cold, in slices.

1 lb (450 g) minced beef
1 lb (450 g) minced ham
8 oz (225 g) fresh white breadcrumbs
3 eggs
A pinch of grated nutmeg
$1/2$ teaspoon ground mace
Salt and pepper

Mix together the minced beef, minced ham and the breadcrumbs so that they are well combined.

Beat the eggs and add the seasonings.

Stir the eggs into the meat mixture.

Grease a 2 lb (900 g) loaf tin.

Put the mixture into the tin.

Cover the tin with foil and stand it in a roasting tin with hot water to come halfway up its sides.

Bake for $1^1/2$ hours.

Leave until completely cold before turning out.

Oven: 350°F/180°C Gas Mark 4

A FRICACEE OF VEAL

Serves 4-6

Fricacee is an old spelling of today's culinary term fricassee, which means meat cut up and stewed in a sauce.

2 lbs (1 kg) lean boned veal
A little lard
2 onions
$^1/_2$ teaspoon thyme
$^1/_2$ teaspoon marjoram
$^1/_2$ teaspoon parsley
A few whole white peppercorns
3 cloves
$^3/_4$ pint (450 ml/ 2 cups) stock or water
1 oz (25 g) butter
$^1/_2$ pint (300 ml/ 1$^1/_4$ cups) white wine
2 egg yolks
3 tablespoons single cream
The juice of half an orange

Cut the veal into 2 inch (5 cm) cubes and put into a large saucepan with the lard.

Fry on all sides to brown the meat.

Slice the onions and add to the saucepan.

Add the herbs, peppercorns, cloves and the stock.

Bring to the boil and simmer for about 1$^1/_2$ hours or until the meat is tender.

Strain the stock and juices and reserve.

Keep the meat warm.

Put the butter, wine and stock into the saucepan.

Bring to the boil and boil rapidly for about 10 minutes to reduce the liquid.

Reduce the heat.

Beat the egg yolks and the cream together and add them gradually to the stock, being careful that the mixture does not curdle.

Add the veal and stir until the meat is completely covered with sauce.

Add the orange juice just before serving.

HODGE PODGE

Hodge Podge is a kind of stew using meat and vegetables. Variations use different kinds of meat. The stew is thickened by the use of root vegetables and is cooked slowly for a long period of time.

2 lbs (1 kg) shoulder of veal
2 or 3 thin ribs of beef
4 onions
6 sticks of celery
12 oz (350 g) carrots
4 oz (100 g) turnips
$^3/_4$ pint (450 ml/ 2 cups) stock

Put the veal and the ribs of beef into a large ovenproof dish with a lid.

Slice the carrots and celery.

Peel and chop the onions.

Dice the turnips.

Add the vegetables to the dish with the meat.

Pour the stock over.

Cover with the lid tightly.

Cook in the oven for 2 hours.

If the gravy in the casserole has not thickened by then, add a little cornflour, keeping the meat warm while you are doing this.

Oven: 300°F/150°C Gas Mark 2

DORSET DELIGHT

For the pastry:
6 oz (175 g) plain flour
3 oz (75 g) butter
$^1/_2$ teaspoon salt

For the filling:
4 oz (100 g) cooked ham
3 eggs
$^1/_4$ pint (150 ml/ $^2/_3$ cup) milk
$^1/_4$ pint (150 ml/ $^2/_3$ cup) single cream
2 teaspoons cornflour
Salt and pepper

To make the pastry:

Rub the flour and butter together until the mixture resembles breadcrumbs. Add the salt and mix well.

Add enough cold water to make a soft dough.

Roll out the pastry and line a pie dish.

Bake blind in a hot oven for 10 minutes.

To make the filling:

Put the ham in the bottom of the partly baked pastry case.

Break two of the eggs on top of the ham.

Mix together the cornflour, the remaining egg, the milk and the cream. Season to taste with salt and pepper.

Spread the custard mixture over the ham and eggs.

Return the dish to the oven for 20 minutes at the lower temperature.

Oven: 425°F/220°C Gas Mark 7
Reduce to: 400°F/200°C Gas Mark 6

FRIED PIG'S BRAINS

A set of pig's brains
Cold water
$^1/_2$ teaspoon salt
2 onions
Oil or fat for frying

Put the pig's brains into a bowl of cold water.

Add the salt.

Leave for about 1 hour.

Chop the onions and fry them until they are soft but not brown.

Strain the brains and remove their skin.

Add the brains to the onions in the pan.

Fry them both until golden brown.

Serve with bread or toast.

BACON ROLY-POLY

For the suet crust pastry:
8 oz (225 g) self-raising flour
4 oz (100 g) suet
$^1/_4$ pint (150 ml/ $^2/_3$ cup) water

For the filling:
8 oz (225 g) collar bacon
1 onion
2 apples
A pinch of sage

To make the suet crust pastry:

Mix the flour and the suet together.

Add the water and mix to make a soft dough.

Roll the dough out to make a rectangular shape about $^1/_2$ inch (1 cm) thick.

To make the filling:

Slice the onion.

Chop and slice the bacon.

Peel, core and slice the apples.

Put the bacon, onion and apple on to the pastry.

Sprinkle with the sage.

Roll up the dough and its filling like a swiss roll.

Wrap in greaseproof paper, then foil.

Steam for 2 to $2^1/_2$ hours.

PICKLED BELLY PORK

Serves 4-6

Pork was once pickled at home with thyme, bay leaves and salt. Today's shop-bought pickled belly pork must be soaked in water overnight before preparing it for roasting.

2 lb (1 kg) pickled belly pork
1 tablespoon oil
A few tablespoons of water

With a sharp knife score the rind along the grain of the meat. The slits should be about $\frac{1}{2}$ inch (1 cm) apart.

Rub the oil into the skin.

Put the joint in a roasting tin.

Put a few tablespoons of water into the tin.

Roast for $1\frac{1}{2}$ hours.

Serve with mashed turnips.

Oven: 400°F/200°C Gas Mark 6

DORSET FLAN

For the pastry:
6 oz (175 g) plain flour
2 oz (50 g) butter
1 oz (25 g) lard
A pinch of salt

For the filling:
6 oz (175 g) cooked ham, sliced
4 eggs (1 egg only to be beaten)
$^1/_2$ pint (300 ml/ 1$^1/_4$ cups) milk
1 tablespoon semolina
Salt and pepper

Sieve together the flour and the salt.

Rub in the butter and the lard until the mixture resembles breadcrumbs.

Add enough cold water to make a soft dough.

Roll out the pastry and line an 8 inch (20 cm) flan ring.

Bake blind for 15 minutes in a hot oven.

Line the partly cooked pastry case with the ham slices.

Put 3 eggs with unbroken yolks on top of the ham.

In a bowl beat together the semolina, milk, the one beaten egg and the seasoning. Pour the mixture into the flan ring.

Bake in a fairly hot oven for 30 to 40 minutes or until the top is brown.

This flan can be eaten hot or cold.

Oven: 400°F/200°C Gas Mark 6
Reduce to: 375°F/190°C Gas Mark 5

NETTLE BAKE

1½ fresh young nettles
2 eggs
¼ pint (150 ml/ ⅔ cup) sour cream
4 oz (100 g) cheese
A little salt and freshly ground black pepper
A pinch of nutmeg

Boil the nettles for 10 minutes.

Drain and chop them.

Beat the eggs and grate the cheese.

Add the eggs, cheese and sour cream to the nettles.

Season with salt and pepper and a pinch of nutmeg.

Turn into a greased loaf tin and cover with foil.

Stand the tin in another tin half filled with water.

Bake for 1 hour.

Oven: 350°F/180°C Gas Mark 4

CHEESE TART

For the pastry:
6 oz (175 g) plain flour
3 oz (75 g) butter
A pinch of salt
A little water

For the filling:
6 egg yolks
6 oz (175 g) strong cheese
1 teaspoon powdered ginger
A pinch of salt
3 tablespoons milk

To make the pastry:

Sieve the flour and the salt together.

Rub in the butter until the mixture resembles breadcrumbs.

Add enough cold water to make a soft dough.

Roll out the pastry and line an 8 inch (20 cm) flan ring.

Bake blind for 10 minutes in a hot oven.

To make the filling:

Beat the egg yolks, grate the cheese and mix together.

Add the ginger and salt. Add the milk.

Put the filling into the partly baked pastry case.

Put in the oven for a further 30 to 40 minutes at the lower temperature. The filling should be firm and brown on top.

Oven: 400°F/200°C   Gas Mark 6
Reduce to :   350°F/180°C   Gas Mark 4

DORSET PICKLED EGGS

Serves 4

These can sometimes still be found served in pubs as a lunchtime bar snack. Eaten with a bag of crisps the combination is somewhat surprisingly known as 'chicken 'n chips'.

8 eggs
1 pint (600 ml/ 2 1/2 cups) cider vinegar or
    white wine vinegar
A few pieces of stem ginger
A few peppercorns
1 oz (25 g) pickling spice
1 cinnamon stick
2 cloves of garlic (peeled)

Hard-boil the eggs.

Remove the shells and put the eggs in a large jar.

Put the vinegar into a saucepan with the ginger, peppercorns, the pickling spice, cinnamon stick and garlic.

Boil for 10 minutes.

Pour the vinegar over the eggs in the jar.

Allow to cool a little then put the lid on or cover tightly.

Leave for a month before eating.

CABBAGE AND POTATO PIE

Serves 4

1 lb (450 g) potatoes
1 lb (450 g) cabbage
2 onions
1 oz (25 g) butter
A little milk
A pinch of salt
Freshly ground black pepper
4 oz (100 g) cheese

Boil the potatoes until very soft.

Mash them with butter and a little milk.

Season with salt and freshly ground pepper.

Boil or steam the cabbage until tender.

Slice the onions.

Mix together the mashed potato, cabbage and onion.

Turn into a greased pie dish.

Grate the cheese and sprinkle on top of the filling.

Bake for 20-30 minutes or until the top has browned.

Oven: 375°F/190°C Gas Mark 5

MARINADED MUSHROOMS

1 lb (450 g) mushrooms
A little salt
6 fl oz (175 ml/ ³/₄ cup) white wine
A few peppercorns
A blade of mace
Half a nutmeg

A small piece of root ginger, peeled and sliced

Put the wine, peppercorns, mace, ginger and nutmeg into a saucepan.

Cover and simmer for 15 minutes.

Allow to cool.

Meanwhile remove the stalks from the mushrooms.

Put the mushroom cups upside down in a large frying pan.

Put a little salt in the middle of each mushroom.

Heat the mushrooms over a high heat.

The mushrooms are cooked when the middles fill with their own juice.

Pour the marinade straight on to the mushrooms.

Put them into a bowl and leave to marinade for 2 hours.

Serve with fresh brown bread.

POTATO AND WATERCRESS SALAD

Serves 4-6

1 lb (450 g) new potatoes
1 bunch of watercress
8 oz (225 g) tomatoes
3 tablespoons single cream
Salt
2 tablespoons finely chopped parsley

Peel the potatoes and boil them until they are tender.

Dice them and leave them to cool.

Mix the potatoes with the cream.

Season with a little salt.

Slice the tomatoes and line a plate or flat dish with them.

Sprinkle the finely chopped parsley on top of the tomatoes.

Put the potatoes on top of this.

Cover the potatoes with the watercress separated into sprigs.

Serve with oil or vinegar separately.

TO STEW CUCUMBERS

6 cucumbers
3 oz (75 g) flour
3 oz (75 g) butter
1 onion
Salt and pepper

Peel the cucumbers.

Slice them fairly thickly.

Let them stand to drain on a cloth until they are dry.

Roll the slices in flour.

Fry in the butter until they are very brown.

Slice the onion and add to the pan with the cucumbers.

Season with salt and pepper.

Let them stew gently until the onion is soft.

Serve hot or cold.

DORSET DUMPLINGS

Serves 4

This is a traditional 18th century Dorset recipe using local apples.

6 oz (175 g) self-raising flour
3 oz (75 g) suet
½ teaspoon salt
About 6 tablespoons water
4 oz (100 g) butter
6 oz (175 g) demerara sugar
1 tablespoon ground ginger
¼ pint (150 ml/ ⅔ cup) rum
4 medium-sized cooking apples
4 cloves

Mix the flour and suet together with the salt.

Gradually add the water to make a soft dough.

Roll out the dough into a square and cut into 4 smaller squares.

In a bowl, beat together the butter and sugar. Add the ginger and rum.

Peel and core the cooking apples. Put the rum and ginger mixture into the centre of each apple.

Put a clove on top of each apple. Put one apple in the middle of each pastry square.

Fold the pastry over the apples, moulding it so that the apples are completely covered.

Grease the bottom of a steamer and steam the apples over boiling water for 1½ hours.

Put the apple dumplings carefully into an ovenproof dish and place in the oven for 5 minutes to dry the outsides.

Serve with clotted cream.

Oven: 350°F/180°C Gas Mark 4

BREAD PUDDING

12 oz (350 g) bread with the crust taken off
1 teaspoon mixed spice
6 oz (175 g) mixed dried fruit
6 oz (175 g) brown sugar
6 oz (175 g) butter
2 eggs
A little milk

Soak the bread in cold water for 30 minutes.

Squeeze out excess water.

Mix together the bread, mixed spice, dried fruit and brown sugar.

Melt the butter and add to the mixture.

Beat the eggs and add to the pudding.

Mix all the ingredients together so that the mixture is well combined.

Add a little milk to make a sticky comsistency.

Grease an 8 inch (20 cm) square tin.

Spoon the mixture into the tin.

Bake for 1½ to 2 hours.

Serve hot or cold.

Oven: 300°F/150°C Gas Mark 2

DORSET CREAM TOAST

Makes 6 slices

This 17th century recipe is a rather rich version of 'eggy bread' and is also known as Panperdy after the French pain perdu (lost bread).

¼ pint (150 ml/ ⅔ cup) single cream
1 egg yolk
A little caster sugar
Grated rind of half a lemon
6 slices of French bread cut fairly thin
3 eggs
1 oz (25 g) butter
1 tablespoon oil
Caster sugar to dredge
6 orange quarters

Beat the cream and the egg yolk together.

Add a little caster sugar and the lemon rind.

Pour the mixture over the bread and leave to soak in.

Beat the remaining eggs.

Dip the bread into the beaten egg.

Put the butter and oil in a large frying pan.

Fry the bread on both sides until golden brown.

Serve sprinkled with caster sugar and with the orange quarters to squeeze over if liked.

QUAKING PUDDING

This is the early 19th century recipe: '1 pt milk stir in 2 oz flour. Set over fire when it has boiled take it off the fire and put in 2 oz butter stir it till melted, beat 4 eggs with a little salt, nutmeg, a little powdered cinnamon, butter the cloth an hour'.

To make today:
1 pint (600 ml/ 2½ cups) milk
2 oz (50 g) flour
2 oz (50 g) butter
4 eggs
Salt
A little nutmeg
A little cinnamon

Stir the flour into the milk.

Heat gently.

Remove from the heat.

Stir in the butter until it has melted.

Beat in the eggs, salt, nutmeg and cinnamon.

Butter a muslin cloth and pour the mixture into the middle.

Tie the muslin cloth securely and put into boiling water.

Boil for 1 hour.

EASTER FURMITY

Furmity, a popular dish, was made of wheat and mixed with a wide variety of produce, from meat to hedgerow berries, to create different flavours.

12 oz (350 g) bulgar wheat or cracked wheat
2½ lbs (675 g) raisins
8 oz (225 g) sultanas
2½ tablespoons cornflour
1½ pints (900 ml/ 3¾ cups) water
1 teaspoon salt
4 pints (2.25 litres/ 10 cups) milk
1 lb (450 g) sugar
1 teaspoon grated nutmeg
1 teaspoon cinnamon
The juice of half a lemon
Brandy or rum to taste
A little mixed spice

Wash the wheat and the dried fruit.

Mix the cornflour to a smooth paste with a little of the milk.

Boil the wheat in the water with the salt until soft. (The cracked wheat will take about 20 minutes, the bulgar wheat not quite as long.)

Add the milk, dried fruit, sugar, nutmeg and cinnamon.

Cook for 30 minutes stirring all the time.

Mix in the cornflour and stir until the mixture is thick and creamy.

Add the lemon juice.

Serve hot or warm with brandy or rum to taste.

When serving, shake a little mixed spice on the top of each helping.

RICE CREAM

3 tablespoons rice flour
3 tablespoons sugar
2 egg yolks
1 tablespoon sherry
1 pint (600 ml/ 2½ cups) single cream

Mix together the rice flour, sugar, egg yolks and sherry.

Stir the ingredients into the cream.

Heat gently in a double boiler until it is thick, stirring all the time.

Pour into glasses and cool.

BLUEBERRY CRUMBLE

Serves 4

Blueberries are commercially produced in Dorset and this is a favourite recipe.

For the filling:
1 lb (450 g) blueberries
3 oz (75 g) sugar
Grated rind and juice of 1 lemon

For the crumble topping:
6 oz (175 g) flour
3 oz (75 g) butter
3 oz (75 g) caster sugar
2 oz (50 g) flaked almonds

To make the filling:

Wash the blueberries and drain.

Put the blueberries into a pie dish or a wide shallow dish.

Sprinkle the sugar, grated rind and juice of the lemon on top.

To make the crumble topping:

Rub the butter into the flour until the mixture resembles breadcrumbs.

Add the sugar and mix together well.

Scatter evenly over the blueberry filling.

Sprinkle with flaked almonds.

Cook for about 40 minutes or until the crumble topping has browned.

Serve with clotted or double cream.

Oven: 350°F/180°C Gas Mark 4

STIR-IN-PUDDING

12 oz (350 g) self-raising flour
6 oz (175 g) butter
4 oz (100 g) sugar
8 oz (225 g) gooseberries
$^{1}/_{4}$ pint (150 ml/ $^{2}/_{3}$ cup) milk

Sieve the flour.

Rub the butter into the flour.

Add the sugar.

Top and tail the gooseberries and chop them.

Add the fruit to the flour, butter and sugar.

Add the milk.

Mix well together to make a fairly stiff mixture.

Grease a 2 lb (1 kg) pudding basin.

Turn the mixture into the pudding basin.

Cover with tin foil with a pleat in the middle to allow the mixture to rise.

Tie the foil down with string.

Put the basin into a large saucepan of boiling water.

Steam for about $2^{1}/_{2}$-3 hours, topping up with water if necessary.

Serve with cream or custard.

DORSET TREACLE TART

For the pastry:
8 oz (225 g) plain flour
4 oz (100 g) butter
$1/2$ teaspoon salt

For the filling:
2 oz (50 g) fresh white breadcrumbs
8 oz (225 g) mixed dried fruit
1 apple
1 lemon
2 tablespoons treacle
A pinch of mixed spice
A pinch of ground ginger

Sieve the flour and the salt together.

Rub the butter into the flour until the mixture resembles breadcrumbs. Add enough cold water to make a soft dough. Divide the pastry dough in half.

Roll out half of the pastry and line a flan ring with it.

Mix the breadcrumbs with the dried fruit.

Peel, core and chop the apple and add to the mixture. Add the juice and grated rind of the lemon.

Warm the treacle and add to the mixture.

Stir in the mixed spice and ginger and combine well.

Put the mixture into the pastry base.

Roll out the remaining pastry and cover the filling with it, pressing the edges together to seal.

Bake for 30 minutes.

Oven: 350°F/180°C Gas Mark 4

DORSET APPLE TART

For the pastry:
6 oz (175 g) plain flour
3 oz (75 g) butter
1 oz (25 g) caster sugar
1 egg, beaten

For the filling:
1 oz (25 g) butter
1 oz (25 g) cornflour
1/2 pint (300 ml/ 1 1/4 cups) milk
1 oz (25 g) caster sugar
1 egg yolk
1/4 teaspoon vanilla essence
8 oz (225 g) cooking apples
1 oz (25 g) demerara sugar
1/2 teaspoon cinnamon

To make the pastry:

Sieve the flour.

Rub the flour and the butter together until the mixture resembles breadcrumbs.

Stir in the caster sugar.

Add enough of the beaten egg to make a soft dough.

Roll out the pastry and line an 8 inch (20 cm) flan ring.

Bake blind in a hot oven for 10 minutes.

To make the filling:

Melt the butter in a saucepan.

Stir in the cornflour.

Add the milk and heat gently, stirring all the time.

When the mixture thickens, remove from the heat and cool.

Stir in the caster sugar, egg yolk and vanilla essence.

Pour into the flan case.

Peel, core and slice apples. Arrange them on the filling.

Sprinkle the demerara sugar and the cinnamon over the apples.

Return to a moderate oven for 20 minutes.

Oven: 425°F/220°C Gas Mark 7
Reduce to: 350°F/180°C Gas Mark 4

DORSET LEMON TART

For the pastry:
6 oz (175 g) plain flour
3 oz (75 g) butter
1 tablespoon caster sugar
1-2 tablespoons milk

For the filling:
2 large cooking apples
2 eggs
2 oz (50 g) caster sugar
Grated rind and juice of 1 lemon

Sieve the flour.

Rub the butter into the flour until the mixture resembles breadcrumbs.

Add the sugar.

Add enough milk to make a soft dough.

Roll out the pastry and line a flan ring.

Peel, core and grate the cooking apples.

Add the caster sugar, grated rind and lemon juice.

Beat the eggs and add to the apple mixture.

Spoon into the pastry base.

Bake for about 30 minutes or until the pastry is cooked and the top is golden brown.

This tart can be eaten hot or cold.

Oven: 350°F/180°C Gas Mark 4

ORANGE FOOL

Juice of 6 oranges
6 eggs
1 pint (600 ml/ 2¹/₂ cups) single cream
4 oz (100 g) sugar
A little cinnamon
1 nutmeg
1 oz (25 g) butter

Put the orange juice and the eggs in a bowl and beat well together.

Grate the nutmeg.

Add the cream, sugar, cinnamon and grated nutmeg to the egg and orange juice.

Mix well.

Cook the mixture over a gentle heat, stirring all the time until it becomes thick.

Add the butter and stir until melted.

Pour into glasses and leave to cool.

DORSET APPLE CAKE

A popular and traditional cake using local produce.

8 oz (225 g) self-raising flour
4 oz (100 g) butter
A pinch of salt
1 lb (450 g) apples
4 oz (100 g) caster sugar
1 egg
1-2 tablespoons milk
2 oz (50 g) currant
A pinch of mixed spice
Demerara sugar to sprinkle on top

Mix the flour and salt.

Rub in the butter until the mixture resembles breadcrumbs.

Peel, core and chop the apples and add to the mixture.

Add the currants, sugar and mixed spice.

Beat the egg with the milk.

Add the milk and egg and mix to a firm dough.

Put into a greased round 8 inch (20 cm) tin.

Sprinkle with demerara sugar

Bake for about 1 hour.

Serve split open and buttered while still hot.

Oven: 350°F/180°C Gas Mark 4

PORTLAND RICE CAKE

8 oz (225 g) self-raising flour
4 oz (100 g) ground rice
3 oz (75 g) butter
6 oz (175 g) lard
3 oz (75 g) soft brown sugar
1 lb (450 g) currants
2 oz (50 g) mixed peel
1/2 teaspoon ground cinnamon
1/2 teaspoon ground nutmeg
1/2 teaspoon bicarbonate of soda
2 eggs
1/4 pint (150 ml/ 2/3 cup) milk
1 teaspoon vinegar

Sieve the self-raising flour and the ground rice together.

Rub in the butter and lard.

Add the currants, sugar, mixed peel, spices and bicarbonate of soda.

Beat the eggs, milk and vinegar together.

Add this mixture to the rest of the ingredients.

Mix together well.

Grease an 8 inch (20 cm) cake tin and line it with greaseproof paper.

Grease the paper.

Spoon the cake mixture into the tin.

Bake in a low oven for about 3 hours.

Oven: 300°F/150°C Gas Mark 2

PORTLAND DOUGH CAKE   Makes 2 cakes

Women used to take dried fruit, sugar, spices and lard to the local baker who would knead the ingredients into bread dough and then bake it. When housewives later collected the cakes, they paid only the price of the loaf of bread for them.

4 oz (100 g) brown sugar
1 lb (450 g) currants
8 oz (225 g) lard
$\frac{1}{2}$ teaspoon mixed spice
$\frac{1}{2}$ teaspoon grated nutmeg

For the dough:
1 lb (450 g) strong plain flour
1 teaspoon salt
$\frac{1}{2}$ oz (15 g) lard
2 teaspoons dried yeast or $\frac{1}{2}$ oz (15 g) fresh yeast
1 teaspoon caster sugar
$\frac{1}{2}$ pint (300 ml/ $1\frac{1}{4}$ cups) warm water

Dissolve the caster sugar in the warm water.

Sprinkle on the yeast and leave for about 10 minutes until frothy.

Sieve the flour and salt together.

Rub $\frac{1}{2}$ oz (15 g) lard into the flour.

Add the yeast mixture to the flour and work to a firm dough.

Knead on a floured board for about 10 minutes until it is smooth and elastic.

Put the dough into a greased polythene bag or in a bowl covered by a damp cloth and leave in a warm place until it has doubled in size.

Chop the remaining lard into small pieces and work into the dough.

Work in the brown sugar, currants, mixed spice and nutmeg until they have been really well combined.

Put into two 8 inch (20 cm) cake tins which have been greased and lined.

Bake in a low oven for about 3 hours.

Oven: 300°F/150°C Gas Mark 2

DORSET BARA BRITH

This cake is still served in Abbotsbury, a village famous for its swannery. The swannery was established by the Benedictine monks who reared swans for their table. Abbotsbury has a Garland Day in May when garlands are thrown into the sea to ensure a good fishing catch.

12 oz (350 g) mixed dried fruit
2 oz (50 g) sugar
³/₄ pint (450 ml/ 2 cups) cold tea
1 egg
10 oz (275 g) self-raising flour

Soak the dried fruit and sugar in the cold tea overnight.

Beat in the egg and the flour.

Grease an 8 inch (20 cm) square tin.

Pour the mixture into the tin.

Bake for 1 hour.

When the cake is cold it can be served with butter.

Oven: 375°F/190°C Gas Mark 5

DORSET FLUFFY CAKE

Prior to the First World War 'The Cuckoo Fair' was an important event. It was held each year in the town of Wareham as near as possible to 17th April and marked the arrival of the cuckoo, heralding the start of Spring. During the fair cattle were sold, farm hands hired and plenty of traditional local food and drink was served.

8 oz (225 g) cornflour
6 oz (175 g) butter
4 oz (100 g) caster sugar
1 teaspoon baking powder
2 eggs
2-3 drops of vanilla essence

Beat the butter until it is soft and creamy.

Add the cornflour, sugar and baking powder.

Beat the eggs and add to the mixture.

Add the vanilla essence.

Grease a deep bun tin and spoon in the mixture.

Bake in a hot oven for 15 minutes.

Oven: 400°F/200°C Gas Mark 6

LARDY CAKE

This cake used up the odd bits of dough left over from bread-making. The traditional day for making bread was Friday so Lardy cakes were baked on Saturdays. They were always made in square or oblong shapes. They were generally rich, fruity and sticky and had a sticky sugary layer on the bottom of the cake. Lardy cakes sold in shops were displayed upside down to show off the sugary bottom (and to prevent them sticking to the trays).

1 lb (450 g) strong plain flour
1 teaspoon salt
$^1/_2$ oz (15 g) fresh yeast or 2 teaspoons dried yeast
$^1/_2$ teaspoon sugar
$^1/_2$ pint (300 ml/ $1^1/_4$ cups) water, hand-hot
  (Alternatively 1 lb (450 g) already prepared bread dough
  can be used)
6 oz (175 g) lard
6 oz (175 g) sugar
4 oz (100 g) mixed dried fruit

To make the bread dough:

Sprinkle the caster sugar and yeast into the water.

Leave in a warm place for 10 minutes or until frothy.

Sieve the flour and salt together.

Gradually add the yeast liquid to the flour to make a dough that leaves the sides of the bowl clean.

Turn on to a lightly floured board.

Knead for 10 minutes until the dough is smooth and elastic.

Put into a bowl and cover, or alternatively put into an oiled plastic bag.

Leave in a warm place until the dough has doubled in size.

Roll the dough out into a rectangular shape.

Spread 2 oz (50 g) lard, 2 oz (50 g) sugar and 2 oz (50 g) dried fruit on to the dough.

Fold the dough into three.

Roll the dough out again and spread with 2 oz (50 g) each of lard, sugar and dried fruit again.

Fold the dough again into three, roll out and spread with remaining lard, sugar and dried fruit.

Roll up the dough like a swiss-roll and put it into a greased 2 lb (1 kg) loaf tin.

Bake for about 35 minutes.

Leave in the tin for a few minutes, then turn out on to a wire rack.

It is best served warm.

Oven: 425°F/220°C Gas Mark 7

BLACKMORE VALE CAKE

Blackmore Vale was described by Thomas Hardy as the 'Vale of little dairies'. This cake has been associated with the Blackmore Vale hunt for 100 years.

4 oz (100 g) butter
4 oz (100 g) sugar
$^{1}/_{4}$ pint (150 ml/ $^{2}/_{3}$ cup) warm milk
1 tablespoon golden syrup or treacle
1 teaspoon bicarbonate of soda
12 oz (350 g) plain flour
8 oz (225 g) raisins
4 oz (100 g) chopped mixed peel

Cream the butter and sugar together until pale and fluffy.

Dissolve the treacle or golden syrup and the bicarbonate of soda in the warm milk, which should be hand-hot.

Little by little add the flour and the milk mixture to the butter and sugar, beating well after each addition.

Add the raisins and the chopped mixed peel.

Grease and line an 8 inch (20 cm) cake tin.

Spoon the cake mixture into the tin.

Bake for about 2 hours, just below the middle of the oven.

Oven: 325°F/160°C Gas Mark 3

CHARMINSTER CHEESE CAKES

Makes 12 small cakes

Charminster is a little village in the heart of Dorset just north of Dorchester.

For the pastry cases:
4 oz (100 g) plain flour
2 oz (50 g) butter
A little water

For the filling:
3 oz (75 g) butter
3 oz (75 g) sugar
1 egg
2 oz (50 g) ground rice
2 oz (50 g) currants
1/2 teaspoon almond essence

Sieve the flour and rub in the butter until the mixture resembles breadcrumbs.

Add enough cold water to make a soft dough.

Roll out the pastry and cut out 12 circles big enough to line small patty tins.

Cream the butter and sugar together until fluffy and pale in colour.

Gradually beat in the egg. Add the almond essence.

Beat in the currants.

Fold in the ground rice gradually.

Put the mixture into the pastry cases but do not fill right up to the top.

Bake in the oven for 25 to 30 minutes.

Oven: 375°F/190°C Gas Mark 5

DORSET CAKE

Dorset cake is probably special to Dorset and originated because most people once grew soft fruit trees in their own gardens. It was a seasonal treat and the fruit harvest was eagerly looked forward to each year.

4 oz (100 g) self-raising flour
2 oz (50 g) butter
3 oz (75 g) sugar
8 oz (225 g) mixed fresh fruit (raspberries,
blackcurrants, redcurrants, gooseberries,
strawberries)

Cream the butter and sugar together until pale and creamy.

Gradually add the flour.

Add the fruit and mix well.

If the mixture is too stiff add a little water, not milk, or curdling may result.

Put into a shallow greased tin.

Bake for 20 minutes.

Oven: 375°F/190°C Gas Mark 5

DORSET CIDER CAKE

12 oz (350 g) self-raising flour
8 oz (225 g) butter
4 oz (100 g) sugar
3 eggs
1 teaspoon cinnamon
$^1/_4$ pint (150 ml/ $^2/_3$ cup) cider
Grated rind of 1 orange
Candied orange peel

Sieve the flour and cinnamon together.

Cream the butter and sugar together in a separate bowl until pale and fluffy.

Add the grated orange rind.

Add one egg at a time with a tablespoon of flour to the butter and sugar mixture, beating until combined.

Stir in the rest of the flour.

Pour in the cider slowly, beating all the time, until the batter is smooth.

Grease an 8 inch (20 cm) cake tin and pour in the batter.

Put strips of candied orange peel over the batter.

Bake for $1^1/_4$-$1^1/_2$ hours.

Oven: 325°F/160°C Gas Mark 3

MATRIMONY CAKE

This recipe dates back to 1880. Legends about true love and marriage are traditional to Dorset. On Midsummer's Eve girls would put their shoes in the form of a 'T' and say the rhyme:

> "Hoping this night my true love to see,
> I place my shoes in the form of a T."

For the pastry:
8 oz (225 g) plain flour
4 oz (100 g) butter
A little water

For the filling:
4 cooking apples
2 oz (50 g) breadcrumbs
2 oz (50 g) mixed dried fruit
2 oz (50 g) caster sugar
2 tablespoons golden syrup
A pinch of nutmeg
A pinch of ground ginger
The juice of half a lemon
A slice of lemon
A little milk to glaze

To make the pastry:

Sieve the flour and rub in the butter until the mixture resembles breadcrumbs.

Add enough cold water to make a soft dough.

Divide the pastry into half.

Roll out one half and line an 8 inch (20 cm) flan dish.

To make the filling:

Peel, core and slice the apples into rings.

Lay the rings on top of the pastry base.

Sprinkle the breadcrumbs, dried fruit, sugar, golden syrup, nutmeg, ginger and lemon juice on to the apples.

Put the slice of lemon in the middle of the flan.

Roll out the remaining pastry.

Damp the edges of the pastry and lay it on top of the flan pressing the edges together to seal.

Brush with a little milk.

Bake for about 30 minutes or until top is golden brown.

Serve hot with cream.

Oven: 350°F/180°C Gas Mark 4

GINGERBREAD

The gingerbread booth used to be very popular at annual fairs. The gingerbread sold at these booths was hard and biscuit-like, and was often shaped into traditional gingerbread men, also crowns, letters and numbers for teaching children to count.

1 lb (450 g) flour
4 oz (100 g) brown sugar
5 oz (150 g) butter
1 oz (25 g) ginger
5 oz (150 g) treacle
$\frac{1}{2}$ nutmeg, grated
2 tablespoons single cream
1 egg

Cream the butter and sugar together until pale and fluffy.

Sieve the flour and the ginger together.

Gradually add the flour to the butter and sugar.

Season with grated nutmeg.

Warm the treacle and add to the mixture.

Beat in the egg.

Add the cream.

Mix the ingredients together well to make a soft dough.

Roll out the dough.

Cut into shapes.

Bake for 30 minutes.

Leave in the tin for a few minutes.

Turn out and cool on a wire rack.

Oven: 325°F/160°C Gas Mark 3

DORSET EASTER BISCUITS

1 lb (450 g) plain flour
3 egg yolks
8 oz (225 g) caster sugar
12 oz (350 g) butter
4 oz (100 g) currants
¹/₂ teaspoon mixed spice

Cream together the butter and the sugar.

Add the egg yolks and beat well.

Gradually add the flour and mixed spice.

Knead in the currants.

On a floured board roll out the dough thinly.

Cut into rounds.

Prick the rounds all over with a fork.

Bake for about 20 minutes.

Cool on a wire rack.

Oven: 350°F/180°C Gas Mark 4

APPLE MUFFINS

8 oz (225 g) plain flour
1 teaspoon baking powder
3 oz (75 g) lard
2 oz (50 g) brown sugar
3 large cooking apples
1 egg
A little milk

Sieve the flour and the baking powder together.

Rub in the lard.

Add the sugar.

Peel, core and finely grate the apples.

Beat the egg and add to the grated apples.

Add the flour and blend well.

If the mixture is too dry use a little more milk; it should not be too wet, for the apples provide the moisture.

Grease about 20 deep patty tins.

Spoon the muffin mixture into the patty tins.

Bake in a moderate oven for about 30 minutes or until golden brown.

Allow to cool in the tins for a few minutes then split and serve warm with butter and jam.

Oven: 350°F/180°C Gas Mark 4

MACAROONS

Recipes for Macaroons (also spelt Macaromes or Macharoons) can be found in books dating back to the 17th century. Almonds, which were then popular, were blanched and then beaten to a paste with rose water.

2 egg whites
6 oz (175 g) ground almonds
4 oz (100 g) caster sugar
A few drops of almond essence
A few split blanched almonds for decoration

Whisk the egg whites until they are frothy.

Stir in the ground almonds, sugar and almond essence.

Mix the ingredients well together.

Line two or three baking sheets with rice paper.

Put a teaspoonful of the macaroon mixture on to the baking sheets, allowing plenty of room for spreading.

Put a blanched almond in the middle of each spoonful.

Bake for 15 minutes or until the macaroons are a pale golden brown.

Leave on the baking sheets for 5 minutes, then cut out the macaroons with the rice paper and cool on a wire rack.

Oven: 375°F/190°C Gas Mark 5

DORSET KNOBS

Dorset Knobs are crisp, dry, crunchy rusks. They evolved from the custom of adding butter and sugar to the remaining bread dough after baking. The process of making them is long and labour intensive for they are rolled by hand and baked in the oven twice. Locally Dorset Knobs are eaten for breakfast; some of the older generation still dip them in their tea.

7 oz (200 g) strong plain flour
5 oz (150 g) plain flour
$^3/_4$ oz (20 g) caster sugar
1 oz (25 g) butter or margarine
$^1/_4$ oz (7 g) fresh yeast
6 fl oz (175 ml/ $^3/_4$ cup) hand-hot water

Sift the flours together.

Add the sugar.

Rub in the butter or margarine.

Mix the yeast and water and add to the mixture to make a soft dough.

Knead until smooth and elastic.

Put in an oiled polythene bag or in a bowl covered with a damp cloth.

Leave to rise in a warm place for 45 minutes or until doubled in size.

Divide the dough into small pieces which weigh just under $^1/_2$ oz (15 g) each.

Roll into balls and put on a baking sheet close together but not touching.

Bake at high oven temperature for about 15 minutes.

Separate the knobs and spread out on the baking sheet again.

Bake at the lower oven temperature for about 2 hours.

Cool on a wire rack and store in an airtight container.

Oven: 450°F/230°C Gas Mark
Reduce to: 250°F/120°C Gas Mark $^1/_2$

TOFFEE APPLES

These toffee apples used to be sold at the annual Cuckoo Fair held at Wareham.

12 oz (350 g) butter
8 oz (225 g) treacle
1 lb (450 g) brown sugar
1 tablespoon vinegar
12 apples

Melt the butter and the treacle in a large saucepan.

Add the sugar and the vinegar.

Boil for 20 minutes.

Put the apples on sticks.

Dip the apples into the mixture.

Leave to cool.

When cold, wrap in waxed paper.

CRAB APPLE JELLY

Wild crab apple trees grow all over the Dorset countryside. The fruit has been eaten for centuries. It is excellent for making jelly which is delicious with roast lamb.

Crab apples
Sugar (amount depends on the quantity of liquid
    from the apples)
Water

Cut the crab apples into quarters.

Put into a large saucepan or preserving pan.

Cover with water.

Simmer until they are soft and the water tastes of apple.

Strain through a jelly bag overnight or put a fine cloth in a colander over a large basin and tip the apples in to drain through the cloth.

Measure the liquid collected.

To every pint (600 ml/ 2^1/$_2$ cups) of juice add 12 oz (350 g) sugar.

Dissolve the sugar in the liquid over a gentle heat.

Boil rapidly until the setting point * is reached.

Skim off the froth so that the jelly is clear.

Pour the liquid into warm sterilized jars.

Cover the jars when the jelly is cool.

* Setting point is reached at 220°F/110°C measured with a thermometer or when a teaspoon of the jelly put on to a cold plate and allowed to cool wrinkles when pushed with a finger.

APPLE MINCEMEAT   Makes about 4 lbs (1.75 kg)

3 lbs (1.5 kg) Cox's Orange Pippin apples
2 lemons
1 pint (600 ml/ 2½ cups) water
2 lbs (1 kg) sultanas
1½ lbs (675 g) brown sugar
½ teaspoon mixed spice
1 teaspoon almond essence

Peel, core and dice the apples.

Finely grate the rind from the lemons.

Put the apples, lemon rind and sultanas in a large saucepan or preserving pan.

Add the water and cook gently for 10-20 minutes until the apples are soft.

Add the spice, sugar and juice of 1 lemon.

Bring to the boil and boil for 20 minutes.

Allow to cool, then add the almond essence.

Pour into warm sterilized jars.

Cover with circles of greaseproof paper.

Seal and keep until needed.

DAMSON CHEESE   Makes about 2 lbs (900 g)

This is one of the oldest of all country recipes. It is a thick fruit pureé and should be very deep purple in colour. The addition of the kernels gives the cheese an almond flavour. It should keep for years and improves the longer it is kept. It is at its best when it has shrunk a little from the sides of the jar. In this condition the cheese was often served as a dessert on a plate covered with split almonds and with port wine poured over it.

2 lbs (1 kg) damsons
Sugar-about 1-1½ lbs (450 g-675 g) depending on the
   weight of the damson pulp
Brandy

Put the damsons in an earthenware dish.

Cook them slowly for about 30 minutes in a low oven until the juices run out of the fruit and the stones are loose.

Remove the stones.

Pureé the damsons or rub them through a wire sieve.

Weigh the pulp and add the same weight of sugar.

Crack the stones, remove the kernels and add them to the damson pulp.

Boil the damsons and the sugar until the mixture is very jelly-like.

Strain and remove the kernels.

Pour into warm, sterilized jars.

Put a circle of greaseproof paper soaked in brandy on the cheese.

Seal the jars and keep in a cool place.

Oven: 300°F/150°C Gas Mark 2

GOOSEBERRY MARMALADE

Makes about 3 lbs (1.5 kg)

2 lbs (1 kg) gooseberries
2 lbs (1 kg) sugar
Water

Top and tail the gooseberries.

Chop them into small pieces.

Put the sugar in a large preserving pan.

Add just enough water to dissolve the sugar.

Add the gooseberries.

Bring to the boil and boil until the gooseberries are soft and have lost their shape.

If necessary remove some of the liquid.

Boil again until the mixture is thick and setting point is reached. (To test for setting point, drop a teaspoonful of the marmalade on to a cold saucer. If setting point has been reached the mixture will gel and wrinkle when pushed with a finger).

Put into warm, sterilized jars and cover when the preserve has cooled.

APPLE AND TOMATO CHUTNEY

Makes about 3 lbs (1.5 kg)

1 lb (450 g) tomatoes
1½ lbs (675 g) apples
6 oz (175 g) raisins
2 onions
1 green pepper
1¼ lbs (575 g) brown sugar
1 tablespoon salt
1 teaspoon mixed spice
1 pint (600 ml/ 2½ cups) white wine vinegar

Blanch the tomatoes in boiling water, then remove the skins and chop them.

Peel, core and chop the apples.

Chop the green pepper.

Mince the raisins.

Chop the onions.

Put the vinegar, mixed spice, sugar and salt into a large saucepan.

Bring to the boil.

Add the rest of the ingredients.

Cook gently, stirring from time to time, until a well-blended thick mixture is obtained.

Pour the chutney into warm sterilized jars.

Seal and keep in a cool dark place until needed.

CUCUMBER VINEGAR

8 cucumbers
1 pint (600 ml/ 2½ cups) white wine vinegar
1 onion
2 shallots
1 garlic clove
A little cayenne pepper
Salt
5 tablespoons milk

Peel and slice the cucmbers.

Put them in a large bowl.

Add the vinegar.

Slice the onion and add to the cucumbers and vinegar.

Add the shallots, the garlic clove, a pinch of cayenne pepper and a tablespoon of salt.

Leave in a cool place for 4 days.

Rub the mixture through a sieve.

Boil the milk and add to the strained liquid.

Leave for 3 hours.

Strain through a jelly bag until it is perfectly fine.

Pour into small bottles and seal.

WATERCRESS SAUCE

1 bunch watercress
1 tablespoon lemon juice
$^1/_4$ pint (150 ml/ $^2/_3$ cup) mayonnaise
1 teaspoon sugar

For the mayonnaise:
1 egg yolk
$^1/_4$ pint (150 ml/ $^2/_3$ cup) oil
1 tablespoon lemon juice

Wash the watercress, discarding any yellow leaves and coarse stalks.

Chop the watercress finely and mix with lemon juice and sugar.

Add the mayonnaise.

To make the mayonnaise:

Keep both the ingredients and the utensils cool.

Beat the egg yolk. Pour in the oil slowly, drop by drop, beating quickly without stopping until the mayonnaise begins to thicken.

The oil may then be added 1 tablespoon at a time.

When the mayonnaise is very thick, add the lemon juice, this will make it thin again.

Keep adding the oil, one tablespoon at a time and keep whisking. The mayonnaise should be fairly thick.

If the oil and egg start to separate, quickly add a few drops of boiling water and then carry on as before whisking very quickly and adding the oil very slowly.

The mayonnaise should keep for a week or more in the fridge.

WALNUT CATCHUP

This recipe was enormously popular in the 19th century. The walnuts should be full grown but quite green and still soft right through, the shells not having yet formed. The catchup was made in July and was thought to be excellent for the digestion.

50 of the largest nuts
2 oz (50 g) shallots
4 oz (100 g) salt
³/₄ pint (450 ml/ 2 cups) white wine vinegar
2 oz (50 g) anchovies
1 nutmeg, sliced
A little mace
A whole peppercorn

Prick the walnuts with a pin.

Cut them into pieces and put them in a stone jar.

Finely chop the shallots and add to the walnuts.

Pound them together with the salt and the vinegar.

Leave in a cool place for a week, stirring two or three times a day.

Strain through a flannel bag two or three times.

Put the mixture into a saucepan.

Add the anchovies, nutmeg, mace and peppercorn.

Bring the mixture to the boil then scum the top.

Boil it for a few minutes.

Leave to cool.

Put it into bottles but do not cork it for 2 or 3 days.

Keep in a dry place.

POSSET

A posset was a drink served in glasses. There are many different recipes for possets ranging from simply heated and flavoured milk, to hot buttered posset using butter, cream, ale, sugar and sherry. This recipe uses white wine.

1 pint (600 ml/ 2¹/₂ cups) single cream
¹/₂ pint (300 ml/ 1¹/₄ cups) white wine
2 lemons
2 egg whites

Heat the cream gently.

Add the white wine.

Grate the rind from the lemons and add to the liquids.

Leave on a low heat for 20-30 minutes or until the posset has thickened.

Remove from the heat.

Whip the egg whites lightly and add to the posset.

Serve warm in glasses.

BLACKBERRY WINE

5 lbs (2.25 kg) blackberries
8 pints (4.5 litres) cold water
3 lbs (1.4 kg) loaf sugar

Put the blackberries into a large bowl and cover with cold water.

Cover the bowl with a cloth and leave for three days.

Rub the blackberries and the juice through muslin to strain out the pips and make a pulp.

Return the pulp to the bowl and add the sugar.

Stir well.

Cover the bowl again and leave for 2 weeks.

Pour the mixture into bottles and cork tightly.

Leave in a dry place for 1 year.

GINGER WINE

This is an old 19th century Dorset recipe which cost 11d to make.

3 drams essence ginger
3 drams essence cayenne
1d pennyworth burnt sugar
1d pennyworth essence of lemon
1 oz (25 g) of tartaric acid

Put 3 quarts of boiling water to 2 lbs (1 kg) of demerara sugar and when cold add the ingredients.

Stir well and bottle ready to drink.

GINGER BEER

Makes about 8 pints (4.5 litres)

This drink was popular with farm workers, especially during harvest time.

1 gallon/ 8 pints (4.5 litres) water
1 oz (25 g) bruised ginger
1 lb (450 g) sugar
1 lemon, sliced
1 oz (25 g) cream of tartar
1 oz (25 g) fresh yeast

Put the water, sugar, bruised ginger, cream of tartar and lemon in a large saucepan or fireproof container.

Bring to the boil.

Cool.

When the beer is lukewarm, crumble in the yeast.

Strain and put in a warm place for 24 hours to ferment.

Put in bottles and stopper securely.

METHEGLIN   Makes about 8 pints (4.5 litres)

Metheglin is honey-based, like mead, but somewhat more spicey
and herbal.

5 lbs (2.25 kg) honey
8 pints (4.5 litres) water
The juice and thinly peeled rind of 1 orange
A sprig of rosemary
A sprig of marjoram
A small piece of ginger root
$^1/_4$ oz (20 g) fresh baker's yeast

Put the water, orange rind, rosemary, marjoram and ginger
root into a large saucepan.

Bring to the boil and simmer for 30 minutes.

Strain the liquid.

Pour the strained liquid on to the honey.

Stir until the honey has dissolved.

Leave the liquid until it is hand-hot.

Add the orange juice and the yeast.

Cover and leave to ferment for 24 hours.

Pour into a fermentation jar with an airlock.

Leave in a warm place to finish fermenting.

Leave in a cool place for at least 3 weeks.

Pour into jars and store.

CIDER PUNCH

4 pints (2.25 litres/ 10 cups) cider
½ pint (300 ml/ 1¼ cups) gin (or vodka)
8 fl oz (250 ml/ 1 cup) sherry
2 oranges
1 lemon
2 oz (50 g) caster sugar
A few sprigs of fresh mint
Soda to taste
Ice

In a punch bowl mix the cider, gin and the sherry.

Add the sugar.

Slice the fruit and add to the punch.

Crush the mint and add to the punch.

Chill well.

Just before serving add the soda to taste. Try about 2 pints
(1.15 litres/ 5 cups).

Serve with ice.

TO CURE ONE THAT IS DEAF

Take 9 house snails and prick them full of holes and set them by the fire upon a plate and then will come an oyle from them wipe it up cleane with black wool then make some more and drop 5 or 6 drops into the ears and keep them close stopped with wool.

When it is dry make more fresh ...

MRS TURSE'S RECEIPT TO CURE FEATHERS FOR A BED

Take the feathers and put them into paper bags. Then into an oven after the bread has been drawn some time. Let them remain all night there. This must be repeated once more then cut off the sharp ends and they are fit for immediate use.

THE COUNTRY RECIPE SERIES

Available now @ £1.95 each

Cambridgeshire
Devon
Dorset
Hampshire
Kent
Somerset
Sussex
Yorkshire

Coming May 1988

Cornwall
Cumberland & Westmorland
Lancashire
Norfolk

All these books are available at your local bookshop or newsagent,
or can be ordered direct from the publisher. Just tick the titles you
require and fill in the form below. Prices and availability subject to
change without notice.

Ravette Limited, 3 Glenside Estate, Star Road, Partridge Green,
Horsham, West Sussex, RH13 8RA

Please send a cheque or postal order, and allow the following for
postage and packing. UK 25p for one book and 10p for each
additional book ordered.

Name...

Address..

....

....

Acknowlegements:

Grateful thanks are extended to the many people of Dorset who have contributed towards this collection of recipes, including:

Dorset Record Office for Quaking Pudding, To cure one that is deaf, Ginger Wine and Mrs. Turse's Receipt to cure feathers for a bed.

Mrs. Stickland for Dorset Cake.

Miss J. White for Easter Furmity.